TRANSPORTATION STATION™

MOTORCYCLES
on the Move

Willow Clark

PowerKiDS press™

New York

For Dan, who was born to be wild

Published in 2010 by The Rosen Publishing Group, Inc.
29 East 21st Street, New York, NY 10010

First Edition

Editor: Nicole Pristash
Book Design: Kate Laczynski
Photo Researcher: Jessica Gerweck

Photo Credits: Cover, pp. 1, 4, 8, 12, 16 Shutterstock.com; p. 6 Haynes Archive/Popperfoto/ Getty Images; p. 10 Carlos Davila/Getty Images; pp. 14–15 Fredrik Clement/Getty Images; p. 18 Robert Cianflone/Getty Images; p. 20 Jeff J. Mitchell/Getty Images.

Library of Congress Cataloging-in-Publication Data

Clark, Willow.
  Motorcycles on the move / Willow Clark. — 1st ed.
      p. cm. — (Transportation station)
  Includes index.
  ISBN 978-1-4358-9335-1 (library binding) — ISBN 978-1-4358-9758-8 (pbk.) — ISBN 978-1-4358-9759-5 (6-pack)
  1. Motorcycles—Juvenile literature. I. Title.
  TL440.15.C53 2010
  629.227'5—dc22
                                          2009026807

Manufactured in the United States of America

CPSIA Compliance Information: Batch #WW10PK: For Further Information contact Rosen Publishing, New York, New York at 1-800-237-9932

Contents

Get Your Motor Running! 5

Motorcycles Then and Now 7

How Motorcycles Work 9

Cruising the Streets 11

Wild Choppers 13

Information Station 14

Off-Road Biking 17

Superbikes 19

Going Electric 21

Motorcycles in Our World 22

Glossary 23

Index 24

Web Sites 24

People of all ages and in many countries ride motorcycles. Here you can see kids racing motorcycles in Canada.

Get Your Motor Running!

Even on the busiest roads, you cannot miss the loud roar of a motorcycle engine. When these fast and powerful machines pass by, they are hard to miss.

Motorcycles are some of the most popular vehicles in the world. People have been riding these machines for fun and for sport for many years. Riders zoom around tracks on superbikes. They **cruise** the streets on choppers. Riders jump hills and ride around twists and turns on **motocross** bikes. If you want to know more, then put on a helmet and get ready to learn about these cool motorcycles!

This is a replica, or an exact copy, of Gottlieb Daimler's first gas-powered motorcycle.

Motorcycles Then and Now

After the bicycle became popular in the late 1800s, inventors started making bikes that did not have to be pedaled. In 1885, a German man named Gottlieb Daimler invented the first gas-powered motorcycle. He did so by placing a gas engine on a wooden bike. Soon, many companies were making their own gas-powered motorcycles.

Motorcycles have changed a lot over the years. Today's motorcycles are safer and more comfortable. Safety is important when it comes to riding motorcycles because a rider can be badly hurt in a fall. Many states have laws that say riders must wear helmets at all times.

Many motorcycles, such as this one, have chrome on certain parts. Chrome is a shiny metal that looks nice and is easy to clean.

How Motorcycles Work

A motorcycle's engine works the same way a car's engine does. Gas from a gas tank enters the engine and mixes with air. This mix becomes a **vapor**. Parts called spark plugs cause the vapor to burn, which forces other parts of the engine to move. This movement is used to power the motorcycle.

Most motorcycles have steel or aluminum frames and wheels. These strong materials are used because they help keep the rider safe. A motorcycle's tires are made of thick rubber that has good **traction**. The tires grip the road while the bike is going fast and making sharp turns.

10 This man is riding a Harley-Davidson motorcycle. Harleys come in different styles, and owners often give the bikes their own looks.

Cruising the Streets

Street bikes are motorcycles that people ride on **paved** roads. A street bike has many of the same things that a car has, such as lights, **mirrors**, and a horn. These things make the bike safe to use while on the road with other types of vehicles.

A cruiser is a very popular kind of street bike. Cruisers have low seats and long, curved handlebars. Have you ever seen a Harley-Davidson motorcycle on the street? Harley-Davidson is a company that is well known for making cruiser bikes. Harley owners often **customize** their cruiser bikes to give them special looks.

There are many ways to customize choppers. This chopper
was painted bright red and given a curved seat.

Pages 14–15: A man riding a motorcycle on a dirt track.

Wild Choppers

Custom motorcycles are motorcycles that have been changed to suit their owners' needs or tastes. Most custom motorcycles are made using cruiser motorcycles. One type of cruiser, called a chopper, is a popular type to use. Choppers are cruiser motorcycles that have been stripped down to only what they need to run. Then, they are customized based on what the owners want.

A person might customize a chopper to give it a bigger engine or a different seat. What custom bikes are best known for, however, are their paint jobs. Many choppers are painted bright colors, with flames, and even with animal prints!

INFORMATION STATION

1 Before gas-powered motorcycles were invented, an American named Sylvester Roper built a steam-powered motorcycle in 1867.

2 The television show *American Chopper* follows the Teutul family, who run Orange County Choppers, a chopper company in Montgomery, New York.

3 The first Harley-Davidson motorcycle was built in 1903, by William S. Harley and Arthur Davidson.

4 Up to eight motorcycles can fit in the same parking space taken up by one car.

5 One of the biggest gatherings of motorcycle fans is the Sturgis Motorcycle Rally, held every August in Sturgis, South Dakota.

6 A motorcycle seat can hold either one or two people. Some people add a wheeled sidecar to a motorcycle to hold another person.

7 There are now motorcycle helmets that can give you directions! A gadget in the helmet gives the rider directions through headphones.

Motocross racers, such as these, must be in good shape. It takes a lot of strength to control heavy motocross bikes at high speeds.

Off-Road Biking

Motocross bikes are off-road motorcycles that are made to handle the jumps and turns of dirt-track races. Motocross bikes have strong frames and tires with excellent traction. These bikes are strong so that they can withstand the jumps and bumps of motocross racing.

Riders in motocross races race their bikes over dirt tracks that are often between 1 and 3 miles (2–5 km) long. Motocross racetracks have built-in **obstacles**, such as wet or muddy areas, steep hills, and sharp turns. To stay safe, riders wear riding boots and special padding along with their helmets.

When going around a turn on a superbike, the rider often leans far into the turn. The rider's knee sometimes touches the road!

Superbikes

A superbike is another type of racing bike. Unlike motocross bikes, superbikes are made to race on paved roads. Superbikes have large engines, high seats, low handlebars, and curved windshields. While on a superbike, a rider sits far forward, which allows him to have good control over the bike's movement. The rider's position also makes the bike more **aerodynamic** as it speeds along the track at nearly 200 miles per hour (322 km/h).

The Superbike World **Championship** is the biggest group of superbike races in the world. It is very popular in Europe, but races are also held in Africa, Australia, and the United States.

In 2008, a police department in Scotland started using an electric motorcycle, shown here. The department wanted to do its part to help the environment.

Going Electric

This book talks about some of the coolest motorcycles in the world today, but what will the motorcycles of tomorrow be like? People are working on making large and powerful motorcycles that use little or no gas. This is important because using less gas is good for the **environment**.

In 2010 and 2011, the motorcycle companies Yamaha and Honda hope to start selling **electric** motorcycles that will travel 31 to 60 miles (50–97 km) before having to be plugged in to recharge. Both companies expect that years from now, their electric motorcycles will be able to go even farther.

Motorcycles in Our World

Motorcycles are everywhere. In some countries, more people use motorcycles than use cars. This is not only because motorcycles are often cheaper than cars are, but also because riding a motorcycle is an easier way to travel through crowded city streets.

People use their motorcycles for many things, whether it is for riding in races, for turning them into works of art, or just for riding around with friends. Motorcycles will be around for a long time to come. The next time you hear the roar of a motorcycle engine, take a look. You will see one of the coolest vehicles on Earth!

Glossary

aerodynamic (er-oh-dy-NA-mik) Made to move through the air easily.

championship (CHAM-pee-un-ship) A race held to decide the best, or the winner.

cruise (KROOZ) To move slowly and easily.

customize (KUS-tuh-myz) To make or change something to suit a certain person.

electric (ih-LEK-trik) Having to do with the power that produces light, heat, or movement.

environment (en-VY-ern-ment) All the living things and conditions of a place.

mirrors (MIR-urz) Flat objects that show exact pictures of things in front of them.

motocross (MOH-toh-kros) A race on a dirt track that has sharp turns and hills.

obstacles (OB-stih-kulz) Things that are in the way.

paved (PAYVD) Covered with something hard and human made.

traction (TRAK-shun) The grip a moving object has on a surface.

vapor (VAY-per) A liquid that has turned into a gas.

Index

B
bicycle, 7

C
chopper(s), 5, 13–14
companies, 7, 11, 14, 21

D
Daimler, Gottlieb, 7

E
engine(s), 5, 7, 9, 13, 19, 22

H
helmet(s), 5, 7, 15, 17
hills, 5, 17

I
inventors, 7

M
mirrors, 11
motocross bikes, 5, 17, 19

O
obstacles, 17

R
rider(s), 5, 7, 9, 15, 17, 19
road(s), 5, 9, 11, 19

S
street bike(s), 11

street(s), 5, 11
superbike(s), 5, 19
Superbike World
        Championship, 19

T
tracks, 5, 17
traction, 9, 17
turns, 5, 9, 17

V
vapor, 9

Y
Yamaha, 21

Web Sites

Due to the changing nature of Internet links, PowerKids Press has developed an online list of Web sites related to the subject of this book. This site is updated regularly. Please use this link to access the list: www.powerkidslinks.com/stat/motor/